Six-Word Lessons for

Executives

100 Lessons
from the C-Suite

Nick D. Anderson

Published by Pacelli Publishing
Bellevue, Washington

SIX
~WORD
LESSONS

Six-Word Lessons for Executives

Interior designed by Pacelli Publishing
Author photo: Pacific Continental Bank

Published by Pacelli Publishing
9905 Lake Washington Blvd. NE, #D-103
Bellevue, Washington 98004
PacelliPublishing.com

ISBN 10: 1-967256-03-9
ISBN-13: 978-1-967256-03-7

Introduction

The path of leadership is rarely a straight ascent. It is, more often, a winding road, replete with unexpected turns, challenging terrains, and moments of profound clarity. It is a journey that demands not only skill and strategy but, more fundamentally, a grounding in principles that endure. Principles that guide. Principles that sustain. It is from this perspective, one shaped by years of walking alongside leaders, and at times, occupying the seat myself, that this collection of lessons is offered.

My own journey has been one of continuous learning, an evolution from corporate roles into the distinct calling of advising and guiding businesses at critical junctures. In 2022, I founded Eighth Avenue Advisors with a singular focus: to come alongside founders and leadership teams, offering not just strategic insights but a partnership grounded in experience and a commitment to their long-term success. It was about helping them navigate the complexities of growth, transition, and value creation, always with an eye toward building something meaningful, something lasting.

Then, in 2024, the opportunity arose to lead OneAccord as co-owner and CEO. This was more than a new role; it was an alignment of personal mission with an established legacy of "Building Value. Built on Values." The vision for OneAccord is clear: to significantly impact enterprise value and job creation, fostering resilience and prosperity within the businesses we serve. It is a builder's vision, one that resonates deeply with my conviction that true success is multi-dimensional, encompassing not only financial metrics but also the strength of our communities, the development of our people, and the ethical stewardship of our resources.

In these capacities, particularly as an interim and fractional CFO and president for multiple companies, I have been afforded a unique vantage point. Stepping into the C-suite, even temporarily, immerses one in the immediate, pressing realities that leaders face. It is a crucible where theory meets the unyielding demands of operational execution, financial stewardship, and team leadership. One week, I might be immersed in the intricate financial restructuring of a mid-sized manufacturing firm, wrestling with cash flow and investor confidence. The next, I could be guiding a rapidly scaling company as its interim president, focused on building systems and a culture that can sustain its upward trajectory.

The spectrum of businesses I've had the honor to advise is broad. It ranges from nascent enterprises with revenues under a million dollars, where the founder's vision is the primary currency and every decision carries existential weight, to multi-billion-dollar banks and credit unions, institutions that serve as pillars of their communities, navigating complex regulatory landscapes and the profound responsibilities that come with significant scale.

What strikes me, time and again, is the universality of certain leadership truths, irrespective of size or sector. The founder striving to make payroll and the CEO of a financial giant grappling with market volatility both contend with the immutable need for clear purpose. Both require steadfast resilience. Both depend on the power of genuine human connection to inspire their teams and build trust with their stakeholders.

One of the most profound lessons learned in these engagements is the critical importance of **integrity**. It is the invisible architecture that supports every sound decision, every strong relationship, and every resilient organization. When integrity is the bedrock, difficult choices become clearer, and trust—that most precious and fragile of assets—can flourish. Another is the undeniable power of **character**. In moments of crisis, it is not merely intellect or experience that carries a leader and their team through; it is the fortitude of character, the commitment to doing what is right, even when it is hard.

I have seen firsthand that **clear purpose** acts as a compass, keeping an organization true north even when buffeted by storms. Without it, teams drift, resources are squandered, and energy dissipates. Conversely, a well-articulated and deeply understood purpose galvanizes effort, aligns disparate functions, and transforms a collection of individuals into a unified force.

The necessity of a **disciplined mindset** cannot be overstated. The C-suite is an arena of constant demand, of competing priorities and relentless pressures. Discipline in thought, in process, and in execution is what separates those who merely react from those who proactively shape their future. It is about focus. It is about rigor. It is about the consistent application of sound principles.

And then there is **steadfast resilience**. No leader, no organization, is immune to setbacks. The true measure is not whether we fall, but how we rise. Resilience is forged in adversity, tempered by experience, and fueled by an unwavering belief in the capacity to overcome. It is the quiet courage to learn from failure, to adapt, and to press on with renewed determination.

Finally, the enduring importance of **genuine human connection**. In an age increasingly dominated by technology and data, it is the human element—the ability to connect, to empathize, to inspire, and to build relationships grounded in mutual respect—that often proves to be the most significant differentiator. True leadership is, at its heart, a profoundly human endeavor.

These lessons, learned not in the abstract but in the very real and often demanding context of leading and advising, form the wellspring from which this book, my second in the "Six-Word Lessons" series, has emerged. My first book, *Six-Word Lessons for Middle Managers*, sought to distill insights for those navigating the crucial, yet often challenging space between frontline execution and senior leadership. It focused on the practical wisdom needed to lead teams, manage upwards, and cultivate personal effectiveness in that pivotal role.

This present volume, *Six-Word Lessons for C-Suite Executives*, builds upon that foundation but shifts the vantage point to the apex of organizational leadership. The responsibilities of a C-suite executive, while rooted in the same timeless principles, carry a different weight, a broader scope, and a more profound impact on the organization's trajectory and its legacy. The strategic decisions made, the culture shaped, the vision articulated—these have far-reaching consequences that extend beyond departmental boundaries, often shaping the very identity and future of the enterprise.

The challenges are also distinct. C-suite leaders bear the ultimate accountability. They navigate greater complexity, face more intense scrutiny, and are charged with making decisions where the stakes are highest. They must inspire not just a team, but an entire organization, and often an ecosystem of external stakeholders. They are the stewards of the enterprise's vision, its values, and its long-term vitality.

This book is designed to speak to these unique responsibilities. The ten chapters, each dedicated to a specific C-suite role—from CEO to CFO, COO to CMO, and beyond—acknowledge the specialized focus of each of these functions. Yet, the underlying lessons within each chapter often resonate across the entire leadership team. For leadership, in its truest sense, is a shared endeavor, and the principles of sound judgment, ethical conduct, and visionary thinking are universal.

The lessons herein are not offered as prescriptive formulas, for leadership is far too nuanced for such an approach. Instead, they are offered as guideposts, as reflections from the field, intended to elucidate the most important considerations for aspiring C-suite executives in their journey of growth and impact. They are grounded in the belief that one can be both ambitious and principled; that success can, and indeed should, be holistic, encompassing not only professional achievement but also personal fulfillment, strong relationships, meaningful community contribution, and the quiet satisfaction of building a legacy worthy of remembrance.

This is a call to a builder-oriented and sustainable approach to leadership. It is about creating lasting value, not just fleeting profits. It is about developing true craftsmanship in our work, building strong communities within and around our organizations, and stewarding our resources—human, financial, and environmental—with a profound sense of responsibility. It is about favoring long-term vision and sustainable growth over the ephemeral allure of short-term gains or disruption for its own sake.

To those who occupy the C-suite, or aspire to it: may these lessons serve as a source of encouragement and insight. Leadership, as I have come to understand it, is indeed a choice—a daily choice to serve, to inspire, to uphold values, and to strive for something greater than ourselves. It is a demanding path, but one of immense potential for positive impact.

As I reflect on this journey and the creation of this book, my heart is filled with gratitude. To my lovely wife, Ariana, your unwavering belief in me, your grace, and your inspiring presence illuminate my path every single day. You encourage me to be a better man, a better leader, and a better partner than I was the day before, and for that, my gratitude is boundless.

And ultimately, all honor and glory to God, from whom all wisdom flows and in whose service we find our deepest purpose.

May these lessons resonate, and may they contribute, in some small way, to your journey of impactful and principled leadership.

Nick D. Anderson
CEO, OneAccord

Contents

Guiding Vision, Shaping an Enduring Legacy

As Chief Executive Officer, your ultimate responsibility transcends daily operations; it lies in illuminating the path ahead and molding a future that outlasts your tenure. This requires a profound clarity of purpose, communicated with unwavering conviction. It is about fostering an environment where potential flourishes, ethical considerations are paramount, and every strategic decision is weighed against the measure of lasting impact. You are the primary architect of not just a company, but a legacy.

Lead with integrity; purpose will follow.

Integrity is the bedrock of true leadership. When your actions consistently align with deeply held values, a clear and compelling purpose naturally emerges. This isn't about crafting a perfect image, but about a steadfast commitment to ethical conduct, even when unseen. Such authenticity resonates deeply, inspiring trust and guiding the organization toward endeavors of genuine significance and lasting impact. Purpose discovered through integrity is unshakable. Relentless.

Inspire with vision; ignite enduring passion.

True leadership calls forth a compelling future, one painted with clarity and shared purpose. Articulate this vision with conviction, connecting it to the deeper aspirations of your team. This resonance builds more than enthusiasm; it forges a unified commitment. People rally to a meaningful standard, their passion ignited not by fleeting hype, but by the prospect of contributing to something significant and lasting. Great endeavors are born of such inspiration.

Connect company mission to personal values.

The most potent motivation arises when the organization's mission genuinely reflects the personal values of its people. As CEO, seek to illuminate this alignment. Help individuals see how their daily contributions serve a purpose larger than themselves, a purpose that resonates with their own ethical and aspirational compass. When work becomes a conduit for personal meaning, engagement deepens, and commitment becomes a powerful, intrinsic force.

Cultivate wisdom; seek diverse, honest counsel.

The summit of leadership can be an isolated place if one is not careful. True wisdom is not inherent; it is cultivated through humility and a willingness to seek varied perspectives. Surround yourself with individuals who offer candid, thoughtful counsel, even when it challenges your own views. Encourage vigorous debate grounded in respect. Such diversity of thought is essential for robust decision-making and for navigating complex terrain with foresight.

There will never be enough time.

Deadlines loom. Opportunities beckon. Demands converge. The illusion of "enough time" is a mirage for any leader. The true skill lies in discerning the vital few from the trivial many. Prioritize with wisdom, focusing energy and resources where they will yield the most profound and lasting impact. This requires discipline, decisiveness, and the courage to say no to distractions, however appealing. Master your time. Master your impact.

You need the very best people.

An organization's strength is forged in the character and capability of its people. As CEO, attracting, nurturing, and retaining exceptional talent is paramount. This extends beyond mere skill. Seek individuals of integrity, resilience, and a collaborative spirit. Sometimes, this means making difficult decisions about those who don't align with the culture or standards. Build a team that elevates the entire enterprise through shared excellence.

Act in service to all stakeholders.

A CEO's responsibility extends beyond the balance sheet to a wider circle of influence: employees, customers, partners, the community, and indeed, shareholders. Strive to create value that is not only financial but also societal and human. Decisions made with this holistic perspective build enduring trust and resilience, fostering a business ecosystem where all participants can thrive. This is the essence of sustainable, principled leadership.

8

Prepare to lead in turbulent times.

Challenges are inevitable. Economic shifts, market disruptions, unforeseen crises—these are the crucibles in which leadership is truly tested. Cultivate resilience within yourself and your organization. Communicate with clarity and calm, instilling confidence even amidst uncertainty. Your steadfast presence and principled guidance during storms provide the anchor that allows the organization not just to survive, but to emerge stronger and more unified.

Leadership is follower's choice; earn it.

Authority may be granted, but true leadership is earned through the willing choice of others to follow. This choice is a profound vote of confidence, rooted in trust, respect, and a belief in your vision and integrity. It requires consistent demonstration of character, competence, and a genuine concern for those you lead. Never take this choice for granted; it is a privilege re-earned each day.

10

Build for the future, not today.

While present demands are pressing, a CEO's gaze must always be on the horizon. Resist the temptation to sacrifice long-term health for short-term gains. Invest in capabilities, talent, and innovations that will secure enduring relevance and prosperity. Consider the legacy you are building with each decision. True stewardship means creating an organization that is built to last, adaptable and resilient for generations to come.

Stewarding Resources and Fueling Principled Growth

As Chief Financial Officer, your role is one of profound stewardship. Beyond the numbers and spreadsheets, you are entrusted with the financial vitality and integrity of the enterprise. This demands meticulous oversight, insightful analysis, and the courage to champion fiscal discipline. Your guidance ensures that growth is not only pursued but is also sustainable, ethically grounded, and strategically aligned with the organization's enduring vision and values.

Guardian of solvency, architect of value

Your primary duty is to ensure the company's enduring financial health, acting as a steadfast guardian against instability. Yet, the role extends further: you are an architect of future value. This requires a keen ability to balance prudent risk management with strategic capital allocation, transforming financial data into actionable insights that pave the way for sustainable growth and enhanced enterprise worth. Diligence. Vision.

Financial resources will always be scarce.

No matter the scale of the enterprise, demands will invariably test the limits of available financial resources. Your critical role involves making discerning choices, strategically allocating capital to initiatives that promise the greatest return aligned with company objectives. Employ data-driven insights for prioritizing investments and exercising rigorous cost control, thereby guiding the company toward its financial goals with precision and foresight.

Master regulations; navigate with ethical compass.

The landscape of financial regulations is intricate and ever-evolving. Mastery of these rules is essential, not merely for compliance, but as a bulwark for the company's reputation and stability. Approach this complexity with an unwavering ethical compass, ensuring that all financial practices are transparent and beyond reproach. This builds trust with all stakeholders and safeguards the organization's long-term integrity.

14

Data-driven decisions illuminate best path.

While experience and intuition have their place, the most reliable financial strategies are built upon a foundation of robust data. Champion a culture where analytics inform every significant financial decision. Seek out reliable data, analyze it with rigor, and use these insights to challenge assumptions and illuminate the optimal path forward. This disciplined approach minimizes costly errors and uncovers hidden opportunities.

Every business decision has financial implications.

Ensure financial thinking permeates every facet of the organization. Collaborate across departments, offering insights into the financial consequences of operational choices, market strategies, and innovation efforts. Foster a wider understanding that sound financial health underpins all success. Instilling this fiscal awareness empowers the entire organization to contribute to sustainable value creation. Prudence. Partnership.

Manage resources with long-term strategy.

The allure of short-term gains can be strong, yet true financial stewardship demands a focus on the enduring strategic vision. Evaluate investment opportunities and allocate resources not just for immediate impact, but for their contribution to the company's long-range goals and resilience. Implement robust financial controls to ensure the judicious management of assets and expenditures, fostering sustainable success.

17

Transparent reporting builds essential investor trust.

Investors and stakeholders require a clear, honest, and consistent view of the company's financial performance and trajectory. Your presentations should be compelling, show-casing growth and addressing challenges transparently. Cultivate open communi-cation, building relationships on credibility and regular updates. Transparency is fundamental for retaining the confidence essential for long-term strategic support.

18

Cost management creates margin, fuels ambition.

Diligent cost management is not about indiscriminate cutting; it's about optimizing resources to create the financial margin necessary for strategic investment and growth. Implement measures that enhance efficiency while preserving quality. Strive for prudence in procurement, production, and operational processes. By thoughtfully stewarding expenditures, you enable the company to fuel its ambitions and enhance its competitive strength.

Say no politely; protect core priorities.

As CFO, you will often face requests that, while well-intentioned, may divert resources from core strategic priorities or introduce undue risk. Learning to decline such requests with grace and clarity is essential. A polite "No," grounded in sound financial reasoning and a commitment to the company's overarching goals, protects vital initiatives and maintains focus on what truly matters for long-term success.

20

Ethical finance: the unshakeable business foundation.

Beyond compliance, a profound commitment to ethical financial practices must be woven into the company's DNA. Champion integrity in every transaction, report, and forecast. Regularly review and audit financial practices to ensure they meet the highest standards. This unwavering dedication to ethical conduct not only safeguards the company's reputation but also builds a culture of trust that is, itself, an invaluable asset.

Orchestrating Excellence and Building Resilient Systems

As Chief Operating Officer, you are the conductor of the organization's daily efforts, translating strategic vision into tangible reality. Your focus is on the elegant efficiency of systems, the seamless execution of processes, and the cultivation of a culture that consistently delivers excellence. This requires a deep understanding of operational intricacies, a relentless pursuit of improvement, and the ability to build resilient frameworks that support sustained growth and adaptability.

Translate strategy into seamless daily execution.

The COO's crucial role is to bridge the gap between high-level strategy and ground-level execution. This involves designing and refining operational frameworks that ensure every team member understands their contribution to the broader goals. Your leadership ensures that daily activities are not just busywork, but purposeful actions that drive the company steadily towards its strategic objectives. Harmony. Precision.

22

Let machines handle the truly repetitive.

True operational artistry involves discerning where human talent shines and where automation offers greater precision and endurance. Systematically identify repetitive tasks that can be reliably automated, freeing your team to focus on complex problem-solving, innovation, and value-added activities. This strategic use of technology enhances productivity, reduces costs, and builds a more engaged, dynamic workforce. Streamline. Elevate.

23

Build systems to ensure consistent quality.

Lasting success is built upon a reputation for consistent quality across all operations. As COO, you must champion the development and implementation of robust quality management systems. This involves clear standards, regular audits, and fostering a culture where excellence is not just a target, but an ingrained habit. Such systems enhance customer satisfaction and strengthen the brand's promise.

24

Oversee supply chains with diligent foresight.

The integrity of your supply chain is fundamental to operational reliability and customer trust. Your oversight must be meticulous, ensuring dependable sourcing, timely deliveries, and cost-effective logistics. Proactively mitigate risks by diversifying suppliers where prudent and cultivating strong, collaborative relationships. This diligent stewardship supports overall efficiency and safeguards the company's ability to consistently meet its commitments. Resilience.

Efficient resource distribution powers every branch.

Optimal resource allocation is key to ensuring every part of the organization can perform at its best. Assess the needs of each department or branch with a keen eye, prioritizing based on strategic goals and potential for impact. Utilize data analytics for informed decisions, ensuring resources are deployed where they can be most effective. Regular review and adjustment are crucial for responsiveness. Balance.

Enhance productivity through empowerment, not pressure.

Sustainable productivity gains are rarely achieved through mere pressure. Instead, cultivate an environment where teams are empowered with clear goals, the right tools, and opportunities for professional growth. Recognize and reward initiative and high performance, motivating through genuine appreciation. When people feel valued and trusted, their intrinsic drive to contribute and excel becomes a powerful operational asset.

Continuously refine operations; seek constant improvement.

The pursuit of operational excellence is a journey, not a destination. Foster a culture of continuous improvement, where existing processes are regularly scrutinized and new efficiencies are actively sought. Analyze internal performance data to identify bottlenecks and opportunities. Engage your teams in this refinement process; their frontline insights are invaluable for staying competitive and agile.

Integrate technology to streamline, not complicate.

Technology should serve as a powerful enabler of streamlined operations. Collaborate closely with technology leaders to identify and implement tools that genuinely enhance communication, data management, and process efficiency. Ensure that staff are well-trained to maximize the benefits of these tools. The goal is to leverage technology to reduce errors, boost effectiveness, and maintain a keen competitive edge.

Lead through change with clarity, empathy.

Organizational change is a constant in any dynamic business. As COO, your role is to navigate these transitions with a steady hand, providing clear communication and genuine empathy. Articulate the vision and benefits of the change, openly addressing team concerns and providing the necessary support and resources to help individuals adapt. Confident, empathetic leadership ensures smoother implementations.

30

Operational resilience prepares for unforeseen challenges.

Beyond efficiency, build operational resilience—the capacity to withstand and adapt to unexpected disruptions. Create flexible systems, develop contingency plans for critical functions, and foster a problem-solving mindset within your teams. A resilient organization can navigate unforeseen challenges with greater agility, minimizing negative impacts and often discovering new strengths in the process. Adapt. Endure.

Crafting Connection and Sharing Authentic Value

As Chief Marketing Officer, your mandate is to build bridges of understanding and trust between the organization and the world it serves. This is achieved not through fleeting tactics, but by genuinely communicating the authentic value your enterprise offers. Your leadership shapes the narrative, fosters meaningful engagement, and ensures that the company's voice resonates with clarity, integrity, and a deep respect for the customer experience.

Understand market rhythms; anticipate client needs.

A discerning CMO listens intently to the pulse of the market, observing trends and understanding the evolving desires of consumers. This requires diligent research and a capacity to translate raw data into actionable insights. By anticipating needs before they are fully articulated, you can guide your organization in developing offerings and messages that resonate deeply, forging a proactive and insightful market presence.

Build your strong brand on authenticity.

A powerful brand is more than a logo or tagline; it is the embodiment of your company's values and promises, consistently communicated. Cultivate this identity with unwavering commitment to authenticity. Ensure your brand message reflects the genuine character of your organization across every touchpoint. Such integrity fosters deep loyalty, clearly differentiates you from competitors, and enhances your company's enduring reputation.

33

Master digital channels with principled engagement.

The digital landscape offers myriad avenues for connection, yet true mastery lies in principled engagement. Utilize SEO, social media, and emerging online tools to craft comprehensive campaigns that genuinely serve your audience. Focus on providing value and fostering authentic dialogue, rather than mere amplification. Proficiency here allows you to broaden reach and deepen relationships with precision and integrity.

34

Develop content that resonates and serves.

Create marketing content that not only captures attention but also offers genuine relevance and utility to your audience. Use thoughtful storytelling, compelling visuals, and interactive elements to convey your message with clarity and impact. High-quality content, aligned with your brand's core values, does more than enhance perception; it fosters deeper connections and builds lasting trust.

Leverage customer data with utmost respect.

Customer data, when used ethically, offers profound insights for creating personalized and relevant marketing efforts. Employ analytics to tailor your messaging and campaigns to meet individual preferences, always prioritizing privacy and transparency. By demonstrating respect for customer information, you increase the effectiveness of your outreach and build a foundation of trust that underpins enduring relationships.

Manage advertising with wisdom and integrity.

Effective advertising campaigns are built on clear objectives, compelling creativity, and precise, ethical targeting. Design and execute your campaigns to drive meaningful results while upholding the values of your brand. Monitor performance diligently, optimizing for impact and ensuring every message is honest and respectful. Such advertising boosts awareness and generates interest by building, not eroding, trust.

Cultivate genuine community on social platforms.

Social media mastery extends beyond broadcasting messages; it involves a deep understanding of platform dynamics and a commitment to authentic engagement. Craft tailored strategies for each channel, focusing on genuine dialogue and building a true sense of community. Stay attuned to evolving best practices, always prioritizing respectful interaction. This approach amplifies your brand's voice through earned trust.

Align marketing closely with sales efforts.

Marketing and sales teams achieve the greatest success when their efforts are deeply interwoven. Collaborate closely to ensure marketing initiatives directly support sales objectives, sharing insights and coordinating strategies for effective lead generation and nurturing. This alignment creates a seamless customer journey, maximizing the impact of all commercial activities and fostering unified progress.

39

Measure ROI and customer lifetime value.

Scrutinize the return on investment (ROI) for all marketing endeavors and cultivate a deep understanding of customer lifetime value (LTV). These metrics are crucial for assessing campaign effectiveness and making informed budgetary decisions. Analyzing ROI and LTV allows you to refine strategies for long-term profitability and sustainable growth, ensuring marketing investments yield enduring returns. Value. Wisdom.

40

Public image reflects inner brand identity.

The CMO bears a significant responsibility for ensuring the company's public image accurately reflects its core brand identity and values. This requires constant vigilance and a commitment to consistency across all communications and actions. When the external perception aligns seamlessly with the internal character of the organization, credibility is fortified, and stakeholder trust deepens.

Building Trust and Growing through Partnership

As Chief Sales Officer, your charge is to cultivate growth rooted in genuine connection and mutual respect. This transcends mere transactions; it involves leading a team that understands the profound importance of trust and approaches every interaction as an opportunity to build lasting partnerships. Your guidance ensures that sales strategies are not only effective but also ethically sound, reflecting the organization's core values and commitment to creating sustainable, shared success.

Winning strategy aligns with core values.

A truly potent sales strategy is one that harmonizes with the company's foundational values and the prevailing market conditions. Identify your key targets with discernment, craft a compelling value proposition that resonates authentically, and implement sales processes grounded in integrity. Such a strategy not only propels revenue growth but also ensures your team is focused, motivated, and proud.

42

Navigate team crises; emerge even stronger.

Periods of crisis test the mettle of any sales team. Lead with unwavering resilience and thoughtful adaptability. Address challenges with transparency, provide clear direction, and offer steadfast support to your people. These moments, navigated with integrity and care, can forge stronger relationships and cultivate a more profound culture of trust and collaboration, allowing the team to emerge more cohesive.

Lead your team always from the front.

Inspire and motivate your sales team by consistently embodying the principles you espouse. Demonstrate unwavering commitment, profound integrity, and a diligent work ethic in all your endeavors. Your leadership sets the prevailing tone for the entire team, encouraging them to emulate your dedication and strive for collective excellence. Leading by example ensures alignment and drives sustained sales success.

44

Manage leads through building genuine relationships.

True salesmanship lies in the art of building strong, authentic relationships with prospective clients. Prioritize meticulous lead qualification, follow through with diligence, and personalize interactions to demonstrate genuine understanding and respect. Building a foundation of trust and rapport significantly increases the likelihood of conversion and fosters the kind of long-term customer loyalty that underpins sustainable growth.

45

Use data wisely to predict success.

Leverage the power of data analytics to forecast sales outcomes with greater accuracy and to guide strategic decision-making. Analyze historical data, discern market trends, and understand customer behaviors to anticipate future sales trajectories. By grounding your strategies in these data-driven insights, you can make more informed decisions, optimize your approach, and enhance the predictability of your results.

Master principled negotiation; seek mutual benefit.

Develop strong, ethical negotiation skills to effectively close deals in a manner that honors all parties. Seek to deeply understand the needs and motivations of your clients and craft compelling offers that provide clear mutual benefits. Mastering principled negotiation ensures you secure favorable terms while simultaneously strengthening positive, long-term relationships—a cornerstone of enduring sales success.

Measure performance to inspire positive change.

Regularly and thoughtfully assess your sales team's performance using key, well-understood metrics. Identify areas of notable strength to be celebrated and opportunities for constructive improvement, providing targeted, supportive feedback. By measuring performance with accuracy and empathy, you can implement changes that enhance efficiency, elevate productivity, and improve overall sales results in a sustainable way.

Maintain a consistent message for customers.

Ensure your sales team delivers a consistent, clear, and compelling message to every customer. This message must be firmly aligned with the company's unique value proposition and its core brand identity. Such consistency is fundamental to building trust and reinforcing your brand's integrity, thereby helping to establish strong, lasting customer relationships and drive predictable sales.

Understand what truly drives clients to buy.

Cultivate a deep and nuanced understanding of the core motivations that lead your prospects to make purchasing decisions. Conduct thorough research, listen with genuine empathy to customer feedback, and analyze buying patterns with a discerning eye. Understanding these fundamental drivers enables you to tailor your sales approach with precision, addressing key pain points effectively.

50

Integrity in sales builds enduring reputations.

The most valuable asset a sales organization possesses is its reputation for integrity. Champion ethical practices in every interaction, ensuring transparency, honesty, and a steadfast commitment to delivering on promises. Short-term gains achieved through questionable tactics will invariably erode trust. A sales culture built on unwavering integrity, however, cultivates lasting relationships and a reputation that becomes a powerful competitive advantage.

Nurturing Talent and Cultivating Purposeful Culture

As Chief Human Resources Officer, you are the steward of the organization's most vital asset: its people. Your role extends far beyond administrative functions; it is to cultivate an environment where talent is not only attracted and retained but is also nurtured to its fullest potential. You are an architect of a purposeful culture, where values are lived, contributions are recognized, and every individual feels a genuine sense of belonging and opportunity for growth.

Attract, retain talent with compelling purpose.

To draw and keep the right people, develop an employer brand that authentically reflects your company's mission and values. Streamline hiring processes, focusing on a positive candidate experience. Offer competitive compensation and foster a culture rich with opportunities for growth and inclusion. By doing so, your organization becomes a magnet for top talent, ensuring long-term success through its people.

Develop people through meaningful growth initiatives.

Invest deeply in your employees' development through targeted, thoughtful initiatives. Implement robust training programs, establish mentorship opportunities, and provide resources for continuous learning and skill enhancement. Encouraging professional and personal growth allows your team members to reach their full potential, which in turn drives innovation and elevates overall organizational performance and resilience.

Fair compensation reflects dignity and value.

Ensure your compensation and benefits packages are not only competitive but also fundamentally fair, reflecting the true value and dignity of each employee. Regularly research industry standards to maintain this equity. Offer comprehensive benefits that address diverse employee needs, including health, wellness, and future financial security. Equitable compensation is a cornerstone of employee satisfaction, trust, and enduring loyalty.

Manage relationships for holistic company health.

Foster an environment where positive, respectful employee relationships are the norm. Actively encourage open and honest communication, address conflicts with timeliness and empathy, and consistently promote a culture of mutual respect and understanding. Strong interpersonal bonds contribute significantly to higher morale, increased productivity, and a more cohesive, resilient organizational culture where people feel secure.

Navigate labor laws with diligence, integrity.

Maintain a thorough and current understanding of all relevant labor laws and compliance regulations. Ensure your HR policies and practices meticulously adhere to these legal standards, thereby avoiding potential pitfalls and reinforcing ethical conduct. Conduct regular audits and provide clear training to your team on compliance matters. This diligence safeguards the organization and promotes fair, ethical practices.

Unique talents united; achieve common goals.

Recognize that every individual brings a distinct set of talents and perspectives. The art of leadership lies in uniting these unique capabilities toward shared objectives. Foster an environment where all employees are respected, their contributions are valued on merit, and they feel empowered to offer their best work. Such synergy not only enhances innovation and problem-solving but also builds a resilient, high-performing organization.

Lead organizational change with empathy, clarity.

Successfully navigate organizational change by leading with transparent communication and genuine empathy. Clearly articulate the vision and benefits of impending changes, while proactively and openly addressing employee concerns. Provide consistent support and adequate resources to help individuals adapt effectively. Managing transitions with strategic foresight and heartfelt care minimizes disruption and guides your organization toward positive outcomes.

58

Utilize HR analytics for informed decisions.

Employ HR analytics thoughtfully to make well-informed, data-driven decisions regarding your workforce. Track key metrics such as turnover rates, employee engagement levels, and performance data. Analyzing these statistics helps to identify emerging trends, address potential issues proactively, and optimize HR strategies for enhanced organizational performance and employee wellbeing. Facts inform wisdom.

59

Keep your team engaged, purposeful, recognized.

Foster an engaged and motivated team by consistently prioritizing employee wellbeing and recognizing their contributions. Encourage a sustainable work-life balance, celebrate achievements both large and small, and provide clear pathways for growth and development. Creating a positive, appreciative work environment where employees feel genuinely valued leads to higher productivity and deeper overall satisfaction.

60

Culture is foundation; build it intentionally.

The CHRO is a primary architect of the company culture, ensuring it aligns with the organization's vision and values. This is not accidental; it requires intentional effort. Cultivate an environment where trust, respect, and collaboration are not just ideals but daily practices. A strong, positive culture is the bedrock upon which employee engagement, performance, and long-term organizational success are built.

Inspiring Progress and Pioneering Ethical Futures

As Chief Innovation Officer, your role is to champion the spirit of inquiry and the pursuit of transformative ideas that propel the organization forward. This involves more than just fostering creativity; it requires a disciplined approach to identifying emerging opportunities, leveraging new insights, and guiding the development of ethical, impactful solutions. You are tasked with building a culture where thoughtful risk-taking is encouraged, and innovation serves the greater vision and values of the enterprise.

61

Generate ideas, then provide viable solutions.

A vibrant culture of innovation begins with the free generation of ideas, yet it matures through the disciplined development of viable solutions. Encourage your teams to think beyond conventional boundaries but then guide them in rigorously assessing and refining these concepts. Your leadership ensures that creativity is channeled into practical, impactful outcomes that drive the company forward with purpose.

Identify trends with analysis for growth.

Stay keenly attuned to the evolving landscape by identifying emerging trends through meticulous analysis. Use data and foresight to spot nascent opportunities and potential shifts that could impact your industry. By understanding these market dynamics and leveraging such insights with wisdom, you position your company for sustained growth and help it remain adaptable in a rapidly changing world.

63

Oversee research, development with strategic vision.

Guide the research and development process with a clear, strategic vision that aligns with the company's long-term ambitions. Ensure your R&D teams are empowered with the necessary resources and unwavering support to innovate effectively. Your diligent oversight of this process allows for the transformation of promising ideas into tangible realities, driving progress and maintaining a distinct competitive edge.

64

Integrate innovations with enduring company vision.

Ensure that all new innovations seamlessly align with and thoughtfully enhance the company's core vision and values. Weave new ideas and solutions into your strategic plans, fostering coherence and unity across every level of the organization. By deeply embedding innovation into the company's foundational principles, you create a clear and sustainable roadmap for future success and lasting impact.

Champion change to maximize true efficiency.

Lead organizational change initiatives with a clear focus on boosting genuine efficiency and lasting productivity. Introduce new processes, ethical technologies, and well-considered strategies that streamline operations and thoughtfully eliminate bottlenecks. Driving change with a steadfast commitment to meaningful efficiency ensures your company operates at its highest potential, consistently delivering superior results.

Utilize new technologies with ethical consideration.

Stay well-informed about the latest technological advancements and thoughtfully integrate them into your operations where they offer genuine value. Utilize cutting-edge tools to improve processes, enhance productivity, and drive responsible innovation, always guided by a strong ethical compass. By leveraging new technologies with prudence, you maintain a competitive edge and foster significant, principled advancements.

Foster culture of collaboration and creativity.

Cultivate an organizational culture where open collaboration and disciplined creativity can truly flourish. Actively promote teamwork and transparent communication, creating an environment where diverse ideas can be freely exchanged, respectfully challenged, and thoughtfully developed. By fostering such a culture, you harness the collective ingenuity of your team to drive breakthrough solutions and lasting achievements.

Analyze markets for needs and opportunities.

Conduct thorough and ongoing market analysis to deeply understand evolving customer needs and to identify emerging opportunities for growth and service. Use these critical insights to guide product development, refine service offerings, and shape strategic initiatives. By staying attuned to market demands with diligence, you develop solutions that meet genuine needs and capture new avenues for sustainable progress.

Communicate complex ideas with utmost clarity.

Effectively communicate complex innovative ideas and multifaceted strategic plans to all stakeholders with precision and clarity. Deconstruct intricate concepts into understandable terms, ensuring comprehension and fostering buy-in from your team and across the organization. Your ability to convey complex information with lucidity is crucial for successful implementation and enduring organizational alignment.

Innovation serves humanity, not just markets.

While market success is important, the truest innovations are those that serve a broader human purpose. Guide your organization's inventive efforts with a strong ethical framework, prioritizing solutions that contribute positively to society and the environment. Innovation pursued with a conscience creates more than just profit; it builds a legacy of responsible progress and meaningful contribution.

Navigating Uncertainty and Ensuring Steadfast Integrity

As Chief Risk Officer, your fundamental role is to safeguard the enterprise by instilling a thoughtful and proactive approach to managing uncertainty. This requires a keen ability to identify potential risks across all operational facets, develop strategies for mitigation, and foster a culture where risk awareness is integrated into daily decision-making. Your leadership ensures the organization can navigate complexities with resilience, protecting its assets, reputation, and its unwavering commitment to integrity.

Comprehensive risk frameworks protect the enterprise.

Establish robust risk management frameworks that identify potential vulnerabilities across all operations, from financial and operational to reputational. Develop clear strategies to mitigate these risks, ensuring thorough documentation and regular updates to the framework. A well-structured and diligently maintained framework is essential to safeguard the company, ensuring resilience and an ability to navigate unforeseen challenges effectively.

Understand the intricacies of regulatory compliance.

Maintain an up-to-date and deep understanding of all relevant regulations affecting your industry. Develop and oversee comprehensive compliance programs, which should include regular, effective training for all employees. Conduct periodic audits to ensure unwavering adherence and to address any identified gaps promptly. Diligent compliance avoids legal entanglements and builds crucial trust with all stakeholders.

Maintain low risk through financial analysis.

Regularly review financial statements and key metrics to identify and assess potential financial risks. Conduct thorough audits and collaborate closely with the CFO to develop and implement strategies that minimize these exposures. By understanding and acting upon financial data with prudence, you safeguard the company's financial health and ensure a stable foundation for sustainable growth and long-term stability.

Apply ideal risk levels to operations.

Achieving ideal operational risk levels requires careful strategic planning and continuous oversight. Assess each department's specific risk tolerance and develop tailored risk management strategies accordingly. Implement effective controls to monitor and manage these risks, ensuring they remain within acceptable, predefined parameters. Regularly review and adjust these strategies to align with the evolving business environment.

Prepare diligently for new cybersecurity risks.

Stay vigilantly informed about emerging cybersecurity threats and invest prudently in the latest proven security technologies and protocols. Conduct regular, thorough vulnerability assessments and implement comprehensive employee training programs. Crucially, develop a robust incident response plan to address any potential breaches swiftly and effectively, protecting sensitive data and the company's operational integrity.

Assess risks of all new strategies.

Thoroughly assessing the risks associated with new strategies is essential for informed, effective decision-making. Before implementing any new initiatives, conduct comprehensive risk assessments evaluating potential impacts on finances, operations, and reputation. Utilize scenario analysis to anticipate potential challenges and to develop proactive contingency plans, ensuring successful and secure outcomes.

77

Help manage crises for business continuity.

Develop a comprehensive and actionable crisis management plan, ensuring it includes clearly defined roles and robust communication strategies. Conduct regular drills and training exercises to prepare employees for effectively handling potential emergencies. Establish a dedicated crisis management team to oversee response efforts, minimizing disruptions and protecting stakeholders during critical events.

Deep knowledge of insurance, risk transfer

Cultivate a profound understanding of the various types of insurance available and how they can be strategically employed to mitigate potential business risks. Regularly review and update all policies to ensure adequate and appropriate coverage. Work closely with insurance experts to develop effective risk transfer strategies that protect the company from unforeseen losses and enhance overall financial resilience.

Balance quantitative and qualitative risk analysis.

Employ both quantitative and qualitative methods for a holistic approach to risk analysis. Use quantitative techniques to assess measurable risks, such as financial or operational metrics. Simultaneously, apply qualitative approaches to evaluate less tangible risks, including reputational or strategic threats. Integrating both perspectives allows for more effective, comprehensive risk management and more informed decision-making.

Risk culture: shared responsibility, vigilant mindset.

The CRO champions a culture where risk management is a shared responsibility, not siloed within one department. Foster a vigilant mindset across the organization, encouraging open communication about potential risks and empowering employees to contribute to mitigation efforts. When a proactive risk awareness is embedded in the company's DNA, the entire enterprise becomes more resilient and prepared.

Prudent Judgment to Enable Sustainable Enterprise

As Chief Credit Officer, particularly within financial institutions, your core function is to exercise sound, objective judgment in the extension of credit. This demands a meticulous approach to risk assessment and a deep understanding of financial health. While the context is specific, the underlying principles resonate broadly: every leader, in extending resources or trust, engages in a form of credit decision. Your wisdom enables sustainable enterprise by balancing opportunity with diligent stewardship.

Effective credit analysis requires deep scrutiny.

Thorough credit analysis is the bedrock of sound lending and, by extension, wise resource allocation in any business. This demands more than a surface review; it requires deep scrutiny of all relevant factors, understanding both quantitative data and qualitative insights. Implement comprehensive frameworks to identify, assess, and mitigate credit-related risks, ensuring decisions are always well-informed.

Portfolio management balances risk and reward.

Oversee the composition and ongoing performance of any portfolio of commitments, whether financial loans or strategic partnerships, ensuring it remains diversified and achieves optimal risk-adjusted returns. Regularly review trends and make strategic adjustments to balance potential rewards with acceptable, clearly defined risk levels. Effective portfolio management supports broader organizational stability and sustainable growth objectives.

Uphold policy; ensure regulatory, ethical oversight.

Develop, update, and consistently uphold clear policies and guidelines that reflect best practices and all regulatory requirements. Establish a consistent, ethical framework for evaluation and approval processes. Regularly review and refine these policies to adapt to changing market conditions and ensure they remain effective, relevant, and grounded in unwavering integrity. This builds institutional trust.

84

Extend trust wisely; verify before committing.

The extension of credit, or indeed any significant organizational resource, is an act of trust. This trust must be extended wisely, backed by diligent verification and objective assessment. While fostering positive relationships is important, it must be balanced with a clear-eyed view of potential risks. This principle applies whether evaluating a loan or empowering a team with significant autonomy.

Objective judgment is a valuable asset.

Cultivate and guard your capacity for objective judgment above all else. Decisions regarding credit or significant resource allocation must be free from bias, undue influence, or emotional sway. Base your assessments on factual evidence, rigorous analysis, and established principles. This commitment to objectivity is fundamental to making sound decisions that protect the enterprise and its stakeholders.

86

True character assessment complements financial data.

While financial data provides a critical part of the picture, a true assessment often involves understanding the character and integrity of the individuals or entities involved. In extending credit or entrusting significant responsibility, consider past behaviors, reputation, and reliability. Numbers tell a story, but character often reveals the author's intent and resilience.

87

Clear terms prevent future misunderstanding, conflict.

Ensure all agreements, whether formal credit contracts or internal resource commitments, are documented with absolute clarity regarding terms, expectations, and responsibilities. Ambiguity is a fertile ground for future misunderstanding and potential conflict. Precise language and transparent conditions build a foundation for accountability and smoother long-term relationships.

Monitor performance; adjust your approach proactively.

Continuously monitor the performance of outstanding commitments and be prepared to adjust your approach proactively if circumstances change or risks emerge. This requires ongoing vigilance and a willingness to have difficult conversations if necessary. Early detection and intervention can often prevent minor issues from escalating into significant problems, safeguarding assets and relationships.

89

Sustainable growth requires disciplined risk appetite.

While growth is often a key objective, sustainable growth is always underpinned by a disciplined and well-understood risk appetite. As a leader making "credit" decisions in a broader sense, ensure that opportunities are pursued within a framework that the organization can prudently support. Avoid the temptation of rapid expansion fueled by excessive or poorly understood risk.

90

Integrity in agreements builds lasting partnerships.

Every decision to extend credit or resources is an opportunity to build a relationship founded on integrity. Ensure fairness, transparency, and ethical conduct through-out the process. When partners, clients, or internal teams see that decisions are made with consistent probity, it fosters deep trust and encourages long-term, mutually beneficial partnerships, strength-ening the entire enterprise.

Investing Wisely; Compounding Long-Term Value

As Chief Investment Officer, especially within wealth management, you are entrusted with the judicious growth and preservation of assets. This requires a sophisticated understanding of market dynamics, rigorous analytical skill, and a disciplined investment philosophy. Beyond this specific domain, the core principles of your role—strategic allocation, prudent risk-taking, and a focus on enduring returns—offer valuable wisdom for any leader tasked with investing an organization's precious resources to secure a prosperous and sustainable future.

Develop robust strategy; align with goals.

A sound investment strategy is paramount, whether for financial portfolios or broader company resources. Analyze prevailing market trends and economic indicators to create a diversified, thoughtful approach. Critically, ensure this strategy is meticulously aligned with the overarching financial goals and core values of the entity you serve, supporting long-term growth, stability, and purpose.

Thorough analysis precedes profitable opportunities.

Identify potentially fruitful investment opportunities through diligent and comprehensive analysis. Assess financial statements, market conditions, and inherent risk factors with exacting care to make well-informed decisions. Such rigorous scrutiny is fundamental to selecting investments or allocating company resources that align with objectives and a prudent tolerance for risk. True insight follows deep inquiry.

Manage portfolio for risk-adjusted returns.

Actively manage the company's or client's investment portfolio to achieve the best possible returns while maintaining a carefully considered balance of risk. Regularly review asset allocations, making thoughtful adjustments based on evolving market conditions and detailed performance metrics. Such effective portfolio management ensures sustained financial health and underpins consistent, long-term growth. Vigilance. Balance.

94

Monitor performance; adapt strategies as needed.

Continuously and systematically monitor the performance of the investment portfolio or strategic company initiatives. Track key performance indicators meticulously, benchmark progress against established market standards or internal goals, and be prepared to adjust strategies with agility when necessary. Regular, insightful performance monitoring allows for timely decisions that can enhance returns and effectively manage emerging risks.

Effective risk management secures investment stability.

Implement comprehensive risk management practices to identify, assess, and proactively mitigate investment risks. Utilize sophisticated risk assessment models and conduct stress testing to anticipate potential challenges and vulnerabilities. Robust risk management not only safeguards the invested capital or company resources but also ensures the enduring stability required for long-term value creation.

Be patient with long-term investing.

True investment success, whether in markets or business ventures, is rarely a product of haste. Cultivate patience, allowing well-chosen strategies the necessary time to mature and yield results. Resist the allure of short-term speculation or reactive shifts based on fleeting market sentiment. A disciplined, long-term perspective is fundamental to compounding value and achieving enduring financial strength.

97

Ethical investing aligns capital with values.

Ensure that all investment decisions, whether of financial capital or company resources, are guided by a strong ethical framework. Seek opportunities that not only promise financial returns but also align with the core values and societal commitments of your organization or clients. Principled investing creates a legacy that extends beyond mere profit, contributing to a more responsible and sustainable economic landscape.

98

Diversification manages unseen and unforeseen risks.

The principle of diversification is a cornerstone of prudent investment and resource allocation. Spread investments across various asset classes, industries, or project types to mitigate the impact of unforeseen or sector-specific downturns. A well-diversified approach reduces vulnerability to any single point of failure, enhancing overall resilience and the likelihood of achieving consistent, stable returns over time.

99

Communicate strategy and performance with transparency.

Maintain open, honest, and transparent communication with stakeholders regarding investment strategy, performance, and outlook. Clearly articulate the rationale behind decisions and provide regular, understandable updates. This fosters trust and confidence, ensuring that those whose assets or resources you manage are well-informed and aligned with the long-term vision and approach.

100

Legacy is built through compounding wisdom.

The ultimate aim of a Chief Investment Officer, and indeed any leader stewarding resources, is to build a lasting legacy of value. This is achieved not just by compounding capital, but by compounding wisdom— learning from experience, adapting to new realities, and consistently applying sound principles with integrity. Such an approach ensures that success is not only achieved but also sustained for future generations.

From the Author

I hope you have enjoyed reading this book as much as I enjoyed writing it!

Writing this book as a follow-up to my first publication, *Six-Word Lessons for Middle Managers* has been an enlightening experience. Now having worked one-on-one with many CEOs and C-Suite executives, I've learned that so much is the same, and yet the challenges are uniquely different.

As you embark on, or continue your journey of leadership and influence through your work, do so knowing that perfection is impossible, whereas sincere effort with humility and integrity is all that anyone wants from you.

I'd like to thank the Pacellis for their encouragement and support throughout the process (again); they truly are delightful partners!

Special thanks to my friend Matthew Bennett for giving me the honest feedback I've needed so many times in life, including but not limited to the writing of my contributions to the Six-Word Lessons series.

With honor and glory to God,
Nick

About the Six-Word Lessons Series

Legend has it that Ernest Hemingway was challenged to write a story using only six words. He responded with the story, "For sale: baby shoes, never worn." The story tickles the imagination. Why were the shoes never worn? The answers are left up to the reader's imagination.

This style of writing has a number of aliases: postcard fiction, flash fiction, and micro-fiction. Lonnie Pacelli was introduced to this concept in 2009 by a friend, and started thinking about how this extreme brevity could apply to today's communication culture of text messages, tweets and Facebook posts. He wrote the first book, *Six-Word Lessons for Project Managers*, then he and his wife Patty started helping other authors write and publish their own books in the series.

The books all have six-word chapters with six-word lesson titles, each followed by a one-page description. They can be written by entrepreneurs who want to promote their businesses, or anyone with a message to share.

See the entire *Six-Word Lessons Series* at **6wordlessons.com**